How to live like you're already in Heaven

How to live like you're already in Heaven
An Atheist's Guide to Happiness

Other printed works by Murray Langston:

How to Be Happy (98% of the Time) ©2022

HA HA, You're Old! (joke book) ©2021

Crazee Coffee Quotes (joke book) ©2020

Unknown Facts (joke book) ©2019

How to Be Happy (98% of the time) ©2018

Journey thru the Unknown
(autobiography, audiobook also) ©2015

How to Live Like You're Already in Heaven

(an Atheist's Guide to Happiness)

©2022 by Murray Langston

Cover Design by Todd Lampe

Unknown Publishing supports the right to free expression and the value of copyright. The purpose of this copyright is to encourage writers and artists to produce the creative works which enrich our culture.

First US Printing

ISBN: 9798360060819
Printed in the United States of America

Introduction

"How to live like you're already in Heaven"

An Atheists guide to freedom and happiness

I am not a teacher, leader, guru, or motivational speaker out to make money off the insecurities of others. I am hopefully just a "Silly Guide" in assisting others to appreciate life and all the good it has to offer, not tomorrow, not next week, not next year, but today and all the following days.

My goal has always been to enjoy each and every day but as I've aged, it's changed to enjoy each and every minute. And I do.

My inspiration ... John Lennon... "Imagine"

Can you imagine if everyone believed in the statement below?

My birthplace is Earth, My Race is Human, My Politics is Freedom, My Religion is Love.

-Murray

How to live like you're already in Heaven

An Atheist's Guide to Happiness

By Murray Langston

CHAPTER ONE

Welcome to HOEville

HOE stands for **"Heaven on earth"** which is how I seek to live my life instead of following an irrational belief that I am going to a Heaven in the sky after I die.

HOEs prefer to live every day like we are already in Heaven and wish for everyone who wants the same to discover the same joy.

HOEville is a place where it is acknowledged that the existence of god is Unknown. Where the worship and adulation of god is considered a waste of time and energy, when instead, it could be much more useful if such worship were applied to our own lives, and the lives of those we love today, here in the NOW.

HOEs live peacefully in a world without a belief in a manufactured god which common sense dictates makes little sense, bordering on nonsense.

Where we learn to love the good (god) which resides within all of us...which as sung by Whitney Houston in "The greatest love of all"...is "Ourselves".

A love we would be much better focusing on than worshiping a god most intellectually informed people are convinced does not exist.

HOEs share a belief that living in Heaven "Now" is the only way to genuinely enjoy the short lives we have. Always appreciating the wonders this world has to offer, HOEs share a disdain for the lies and confusion so many religions advance in their teachings. I am not saying that everything about religion is abhorrent, but the good it does is far outweighed by the bad it's responsible for.

Being a HOE, you believe the only heaven is here on earth and that it is your priority to live in that heaven to the best of your ability.

HOEs believe that no one is better than us and we are no better than anyone else. Not the President, the Pope, our boss, no one. And we are no better than those less fortunate than ourselves, whether immigrants trying to free themselves from tyranny, or that unfortunate person whose job it is cleaning the toilets at Taco Bell.

We are just luckier than others and we acknowledge, appreciate, and are grateful for the abundant luck we have enjoyed when so many have so little.

It is not difficult to comprehend and appreciate happiness when you consider that if you own a car and a house, you reside in the upper 1% of the almost 8 billion people on this planet. This an amazing statistic that should cause anyone in that group to be grateful, thankful, and appreciative.

CHAPTER TWO

Teeny Weeny Sandwiches

The following is from the Atheist Republic and says much about religion and how nonsensical it appears to thinking people.

It's like this: "I created man and woman with original sin. Then I destroyed most of them for sinning. Then I impregnated a woman with myself as her child, so that I could be born. Later, I will kill myself as a sacrifice to myself to save all of you from the sin I gave to you in the first place."

I used to tell a joke, "I was an Atheist until I found out I was god." Which became the basis for my religious beliefs. I do not look outside myself for spiritual answers, they are within us, and most questions about religion cannot be answered.

How did Jesus feed thousands of people with one fish, and one loaf of bread? The Answer: "Teeny weeny sandwiches." Okay, that's another joke, but there are too many of these unanswerable questions in the Bible, so I leave them to those who need to get a life.

If you feel the need to believe in something, it is far better to believe in the one and only "YOU" than to believe in one of the thousands of Religions, none of which make any logical sense.

Over the centuries, legions of historians much more intelligent than I can ever hope to be, have studied, researched, and tried to produce an answer which solidifies their belief in a god, and so far, No One has. So, I am not going to waste one minute of my life trying to figure it out, and instead, I will enjoy my day-to-day existence without trying to find an answer to the unanswerable.

Most Americans were raised by parents who shared the same religion they were raised on and force-fed their children to believe the same as they did.

I feel fortunate because though my mom was religious, attending church every Sunday, my dad was an Atheist, so as my siblings and I grew older, we were able to choose between these two belief systems. (Interesting to note that all five of us kids became Atheists)

It is my belief historic leaders ingeniously convinced people through religion that they will see each other after they die, a belief that became dominant in the minds and hearts of people thousands of years ago and continues today.

Thousands of years ago, except for kings, designated priests, and their inner circles, people were illiterate and pliable, believing in witches and other absurdities, including the world being flat. Their leaders knew the concept of religion would make it easier to manipulate and maintain control over their societies, the same way our leaders continue to do today and are succeeding.

No one knows for sure if there is a higher power whose purpose is beyond our comprehension, but I am 100% positive that all the religions in the world which are forced daily into the minds of millions of children are bullshit. My Dad believed Jesus was from another planet who unfortunately landed on earth, where he was tortured and crucified before escaping on that fiery chariot, as described in the bible.

If I did believe in Jesus, I would be more inclined to follow my dad's theory than the others. It makes more sense than believing in a god who allows thousands of babies to starve to death daily without doing anything about it. Most religions rely on the ten commandments to control their followers. Commandments are orders from a leader who oversees you, and it is your duty as a follower to obey. This may work for the military who have signed up to take orders, but they do not belong in a HOEs life. HOEs are individuals who have taken charge of their lives and will listen, analyze, debate, consider and in the end decide what is best for themselves and those they love.

HOEs are not followers but prefer to participate in a movement that allows them to fully enjoy the life they have. HOEs do not need to be told to be nice to each other as the Commandments put forth. Being nice comes naturally to us.

CHAPTER THREE

The Ten HOEmandmets

My list of 10 things most HOEs do NOT believe followed by 10 things we DO believe.

You will notice I said "Most" HOEs, because NOT everyone has to agree and/or adhere to these suggestions, but simply have an awareness of them. Because we are all uniquely special with different degrees of intellect, coupled with varying levels of education, we must learn what is best for ourselves and what contributes to our enjoyment of this magnificent thing called LIFE.

Work, any kind of work, sucks unless you love it. And so it goes with Life, which can also suck... unless you love it. I love my life and you can and should love your life too.

"I love Sundays. But I also love Mondays, Tuesdays, Wednesdays, Thursdays, Fridays, and Saturdays."

Most HOEs do NOT believe:

"Either god made a mistake creating man or man made a mistake creating god." (Unknown)

1) HOEs do Not believe in god

It is easy to understand why millions believe god is real when you consider for years, millions of people have believed, and still do that, "PROFESSIONAL" wrestling is real. Your beliefs do not make you a better person, your behavior does.

I am an Atheist, and it does not mean I am bitter, unhappy, hateful or that I know everything.

I am not an Atheist because I am cool, or something bad happened to me or I follow Satan. I'm an Atheist because after carefully analyzing the evidence, the existence of god makes absolutely no sense to me,

"Religion is regarded by the common people as true, by the wise as false, and by the rulers as useful." (Seneca)

2) HOEs do Not believe in Religion

The human brain is an amazing organ that works 24 hours a day every second of every day from the time you leave the womb until you find religion. Once you realize that nothing about religion makes sense, everything will start making sense.

It is not a theory, but a "Fact" that if I had been adopted or kidnapped at birth by a Muslim extremist couple and taken to Iran, I would today be a Muslim.

No matter what Religion you belong to, if you were adopted or kidnapped at birth by a Korean couple and taken to North Korea, you would today believe Kim Jong-un is your God. You would be a product of those circumstances. This is not theory, this is fact.

So how can anyone believe in any One Religion when your religious beliefs are an absolute result of what you were convinced to believe by those who controlled you. We are all a product of the religions that we were indoctrinated into by our parents. And that is a fact. What America does provide is the freedom to break away from the brainwashing we were subjected to, unlike countries under a dictatorship.

However, though we all have the freedom, few possess the intellect.

I was married to a Catholic woman who convinced me going to church would enhance our struggling relationship. When a grossly overweight priest preached about how we should live our lives, I had to laugh.

All I could think of was this guy was telling us how to live, yet he could not take care of his own body. This seemed ridiculous and I have never since attended church. My relationship also ended shortly thereafter.

"The total absence of humor from the Bible is one of the most singular things in all literature." (Alfred North Whitehead)

3) HOEs do not believe in being a follower or the Bible

It's hard to comprehend that adults continue to believe two penguins walked from Antarctica to the Middle East, to get on Noah's Ark along with seven million other species which existed at the time. I would love to know how the feeding and cleaning after all those animals went.

Or the passage referring to the tower of Babel, where different languages began when man attempted to build a tower to reach the heavens.

This frightened god so much he/she made everyone speak different languages so they couldn't communicate, thus making it impossible to continue to construct this tower.

When you consider that millions still believe this junk food of knowledge, it is not hard to understand how gullible humans are.

Within most religions is a leader or leaders with a multitude of followers. HOEs are not followers. Watching church services on TV, led by the likes of Dr. Charles Stanley or Joel Osteen, I am bewildered watching the faces in the audience who are captivated by their hypnotic words.

Words are carefully chosen to convince them they are all sinners who need to be saved from going to hell.

I cannot help but feel they are "sheep" who have little control over their lives, being led over an irrational thinking cliff. HOEs are not sheep.

I think of myself as a "Lion" who oversees its domain and can make its own decisions. HOEs feel they are responsible for their own lives and do not have to depend on religious leaders for their salvation.

People get so caught up in following, they forget they can also lead. HOEs are leaders in control of their lives who are in a constant search to gain knowledge which will enhance themselves and the ones they love.

Religions teach that money is the root of all evil, yet beg for it at every opportunity available. If you are a follower of religion, you must also attend church where you are duped to donate money, which is frequently used to pay off legal fees for crimes against our young by its leaders. HOEs get to use that money for more important things.

"When I do good, I feel good. When I do bad, I feel bad. That's my religion." - Abraham Lincoln

"Religion is like a blind man looking in a black room for a black cat that isn't there... and finding it." (Oscar Wilde)

4) HOEs do not believe in Sin

Preachers constantly remind their flocks "Jesus died for their sins", when he obviously died for nothing. "**News Flash**": people have NOT stopped sinning. In fact, sinning has reached epidemic proportions. If it were not for sinning, (or what is judged as sinning) most people, including yours truly, would have missed out on a lot of fun.

I recall as a kid a priest telling me that if I chewed gum in church, it was a sin. That alone displayed the *absurdity* of sin.

I was also told that if I had impure thoughts about a girl, it was a sin, and I would go to hell. Talk about child abuse! For something as normal for a pubescent boy as thinking impure thoughts about a girl!

I recall watching dogs have sex, not the least concerned about impure thoughts (they're Atheists too) and decided all this sin stuff was impure nonsense.

"Your prayers are always answered and the answer's no!" (Unknown)

5) HOEs do not believe in prayer

HOEs believe in the power of action. With the Trillions of prayers uttered each day for peace on earth, I would hate to see what this world would be like if there were NO prayers.

Seriously, If you were lost in the mountains and given a choice of having 10,000 people praying for you or one person looking for you, which would you choose? The answer is obvious.

"Faith: is NOT wanting to know what the truth is" - (Friedrich Nietzsche)

6) Hoes do not believe in faith

If you stand on a railroad track having all the faith in the world that a train hitting you will Not hurt you, you would be dead wrong. Also, dead. I find these kinds of devout believers to be intellectually immature.

Or, they are so brain washed, common sense does not make sense to them.

I was intellectually immature until my thirties, when I decided to apply analytical thought to religion rather than simply accepting its rules, because I was told to by my parents, preachers, politicians and/or society.

The average person is not responsible for the chaos in the world today or thousands of years ago. It is the leaders of the tribes, communities, societies and countries who have been responsible for ruining people's lives then...and now.

Those rulers learned by enlisting clerics and priests to write an imaginative work depicting a Godlike creator, who put fear into the populace to control them, would work then, and continues to work today.

Nobody knows whether the words written about Jesus Christ 2,000 years ago contain truth or that he even existed.
Though we know some facts about Christopher Columbus who supposedly discovered America in 1492, books written about him have opposing views about his character. Some say he was criminal; others say he was a nice guy.

These writings about Christ or Columbus do not contain a substantial amount of TRUTH to bet your life savings on, much less bet the quality of your life on.

"After your death you will be what you were before your birth." (Schopenhauer)

7) HOEs do not believe in an afterlife

If you think your afterlife will be better than your current life, you are not living, you are waiting to die. Death is simply an end to a fabulous ride and for me, what a ride it has been.

Though I do not look forward to it, I accept death, because I have No Choice. We should never worry about how we are going to die, but how we are going to live.

HOEs accept that the "word" which best describes death is "Inevitable". There is nothing we can do to prevent death so why worry about it, be concerned about it, or even discuss it? The only discussion we should have regarding death is its opposite..."Life" and how to live it to the fullest.

It would be great if after I die, I would get to go to a heavenly place where I'll see my loved ones - but it ain't gonna happen. It would be great if after I die, I came back as the Queen of England, but it ain't gonna happen either. Both are preposterous.

Just as teaching children if they commit sins, they risk burning in a fiery hell is child abuse, teaching them if they don't commit sins, they will find a seat next to god where they will live in paradise for eternity is equally abusing the thinking of young, curious minds.

Believing that earth is a waiting room for a mythical, heavenly place makes no sense.

Believing we can live the worst lives imaginable, destroying our bodies and the world around us, and still get the full benefit of heaven, if we ask for forgiveness and place money in the collection plate, is also ridiculous.

I am convinced that when I die, it is going to be "Lights out." But, I'm going to continue to have a great time while the lights are on.

A wonderful quote about life and death by Vin Scully, renowned sports broadcaster who died at the age of 94...

"It's been a wonderful ride. My last day will not be a sad day. It will be a Thanksgiving Day."

"The best religion is the love of Family, Friends, and Humanity." (Unknown)

8) HOEs do not believe in Destiny

HOEs believe that saying "it's Destiny" is a lousy excuse to wait for things to happen instead of making them happen.

If you believe in Destiny, you will also believe there is no reason to grab the reins of your life and work hard to secure what you want for yourself and your future. HOEs do not believe in what will be will be.

HOEs believe in what will be is what you make it. And rather than accept things the way they are, be able to affect positive change by working hard at it.

When you believe that Life only happens once, you want to make sure you do the things that make you happy and be with the people who make you smile.

If you believe that everything happens for a reason, then you must also believe that there are a lot of stupid people making bad decisions.

Everyone does NOT have a purpose...

Christian author, Rick Warren wrote a hugely successful book titled, "The Purpose Driven Life", about his belief that everyone's life has a God driven purpose, which I believe borders on the absurd.

How arrogant I would be to believe that god gave me a special purpose when over 20,000 children starve to death every day. It makes no sense unless the god driven purpose for all these children being born, was to starve to death.

Or a serial killer's god driven purpose was to massacre as many people as they can before killing themselves or getting captured and spending the rest of their life in prison.

When people say, "Everything happens for a reason". Can someone please tell me the reason?

I do not get this searching for the meaning of life. Why assume life has a meaning at all? You have a life, enjoy it.

The meaning of life is to give your life meaning while you are here and if you cannot do that, so what, if you mean well and had a fun life.

HOEs believe that our sole driven purpose is **two** things.

To **procreate** and to **survive**.

Without procreation humanity would end rather quickly so it is necessary we survive so we can keep procreating, an activity we seem to enjoy. I know I still do.

"Though it's hard to win an argument about religion with a smart person, it's damn near impossible with a stupid person." (Unknown)

9) HOEs do Not believe in hate, worry, guilt, stress, or jealousy

"Hate" causes YOU to suffer rather than the person you hate, who likely is not aware or could care less.

"Worry" serves no purpose. If you have something to worry about, do something about it. Don't let it consume your time or energy.

"Guilt" should only be felt if you purposely hurt someone. If you are that kind of person, you are a sociopath and need serious help.

"Stress" can damage your immune system. Deal with stress like a Dog. If you cannot eat it, play with it or pee on it, walk away from it.

"Jealousy" - It is your partners duty to ensure that you feel secure enough in your relationship to have no reason to be jealous. If they are doing that and you still feel jealous, YOU have the problem. We all feel these emotions but by understanding that each has a detrimental effect on our happiness, we must eliminate them from occupying space in our minds.

When you are feeling down, face it, accept it, learn from it, try to understand it, but never wallow in it. Relax. Mediate. Let go. Chill. Move on. When you focus on problems, you will find you have more problems. When you focus on possibilities, you will find you have more opportunities.

Hatred. worry, jealousy, guilt, or stress will never solve a problem. But love will. So, focus on what matters and let go of what does not. Life should be about Living, Laughing and Loving... and never existing. Try not to live your life thinking people are as nice as you because many are Not.

And if you can find humor in difficult situations, you will always end up a winner.

10) HOEs do Not believe in the Ten Commandments...

1) Thou shall not have other gods before me. (I prefer no imaginary gods before, during or after me.)

2) Thou shall not take the name of the lord in vain. (If I stub my toe and it hurts, I will take somebody's name in vain. Do you ever wonder what the Pope yells when he stubs his toe)

3) Thou shall keep holy the sabbath day. (Holy is a word coined by early religious leaders. Its definition means "special". If that is so, then I want all my days to be special, just like today and tomorrow will be.)

4) Thou shall honor your mother and father. (Unless they are abusive in any way, then they deserve no honor)

5) Thou shall not kill. (If I see someone raping my 5-year-old child, I will try to kill them)

6) Thou shall not commit adultery.
(Unless I find out my partner has been having sex with the local football team.)

7) Thou shall not steal.
(If I am starving and my rich neighbor leaves bread on his porch, then steal I must. But I will return the bread if my life improves.)

8) Thou shall not bear false witness against your neighbor. (If I must lie about my neighbor to keep them from getting hurt, physically, or otherwise, then I will do the right thing.)

9) Thou shall not covet your neighbor's wife.
(If she is abused by her husband, works at Hooters and comes to me for solace, then I might have to engage in some coveting.)

10) Thou shall not covet anything that belongs to your neighbor.
(Seems like 7 and 9 already cover this coveting.)

Some of my favorite Unknown Quotes

"If it doesn't make the world a better place, don't do it."

"Spending time with kids is much more important than spending money on kids."

"It's not that people use only 10% of their brains, it's that only 10% of people use their brains."

"What would be scarier than spending an eternity in hell? Spending an eternity in heaven with a bunch of religious fanatics."

"Life is like a Roller Coaster. You can either scream at every bump or you can just throw your hands in the air and enjoy the ride."

"Yesterday is dead, tomorrow hasn't arrived yet. I have just one day, and I'm going to be happy in it." (Groucho Marx)   (That ONE I KNEW)

CHAPTER FOUR

The Ten Suggestions

Below are NOT commandments but ten *suggestions* (HOEggestions) why it makes sense to live a life with freedom from the binds and ties of religion. HOEs are not asked to adhere to these BELIEFS but may or may not find them beneficial on Life's awesome journey.

(Most HOEs believe)

1) The Happiest day of your life is Today.

"Life is a great big canvas; throw all the paint you can at it." (Danny Kaye)

Since I was a teen-ager, my goal has been to be happy in the now because the now is known and sure and the future is unknown and unsure. Heaven and Happiness have equal meaning to me.

I believe the life we are now living is our heaven and each day is a heavenly day to enjoy. When I awake and open my eyes, I look forward to enjoying my coffee heaven followed by my breakfast heaven, my work heaven, my family heaven, my friend's heaven, and my love heaven for my family and friends.

By living in the present and focusing on experiencing each minute and enjoying it to the max, we truly can feel we are living in heaven.

HOEs do not believe in worrying about the years in front of us, we believe in focusing on the minutes surrounding us. We are aware that Happiness is not something you search for but is a constant in our lives if we want it to be. And I want it to be.

HOEs believe each day is Not just another day but an opportunity to learn, grow, laugh, explore, and experience.

Each day can be the beginning of something new, so embrace them with gusto.

Even if you begin by "pretending" that life is wonderful, that is okay, because you will eventually find yourself no longer pretending.

Happiness happens when you have something to look forward to, whether tinkering in your garden, having lunch with a friend, painting a room, shopping, planning a new project, eating at your favorite restaurant, or simply going to the movies.

Your days should be a feast of senses and emotions, with a buffet of sights, sounds, laughter, conversations and of course, love.

Happiness has little to do with being rich, famous, or perfect. It is about enjoying every MINUTE and not letting the bullshit around you spoil it, because the future is never guaranteed, the past is gone, but each minute is right in front of and around you to enjoy.

I am not saying you should not relish memories from the past or not plan for the future, but they should not be your major focus.

Learn from the past and prepare for the future (a little) but your major focus should always be LIVING for TODAY.

Why Learn to Live for today? We are born in one day. We die one day. We can fall in love in one day. We can change the course of our life in one day. The most amazing things can happen in one day. So Live for Today.

Simplicity is one of the keys to achieving happiness.

"For a happy life, tie yourself to a Goal, not to people or objects." (Albert Einstein)

The more you have, the more complex your life becomes and the increased chance of living a life filled with stress, the result being a life controlled by your stuff, rather than you are in control of your stuff.

Life should never be about Winning or Losing. It should be about having fun and engaging in activities that bring you pleasure and a sense of accomplishment. I always enjoyed winning, but I was always a good loser. Winning or losing should never bring you overexcitement or disappointment, it should all be fun.

Also, keep your problems close to yourself and your immediate family. If you like telling others about your problems, most either do not care or are glad you have them.

I am Happy almost all the time, but I am Happiest when the people I love are Happy. My basic philosophy is: if my kids and I are healthy, both physically and emotionally, I have absolutely no reason to be unhappy, because most everything else is bullshit.

Fortunately, my two daughters and I are healthy and that is what matters. Anyone with a reasonable amount of intellect will admit that without your health, everything else becomes meaningless.

Happiness is not hard to find. It is beside you; it is in front of you, it's at your back, it's around you, it's everywhere. It is just a matter of appreciation. Laugh often and you will enjoy your life. Laugh at yourself and you will enjoy it even more. When life knocks you down, instead of getting right back up, sometimes it is better to just lie there and take a nap.

Peace & Serenity are two other key factors in achieving happiness

NEVER engage in a heated argument. I have friends of 20, 30, 40 years who I have NEVER had an argument with, and I have had friends and lovers who cannot seem to participate in any productive dialogue without arguing. These people should have no place in your life. There is an old saying, "When you argue with a fool, two fools are arguing", and I refuse to be a member of the fool club again.

I am not saying there is no room for discussion. Constructive dialogue between friends, lovers and family is necessary for growth and understanding of others who think differently on issues. But, when it leads to destructive insults then you need to bring it to an end, before it becomes damaging to both you and the person with whom you are arguing.

There is a difference between discussion and arguing where voices are raised to a fever pitch. I have disappointed myself more than once having been there, and you cannot be happy when you are arguing.

If I see an argument about to erupt, I will immediately walk away rather than risk losing my peace and serenity, not to mention losing a friend or lover. Arguments are not beneficial for a lasting friendship/relationship, but to the contrary are a huge red flag that the end of that relationship is inevitable.

Similarly, when a man hits a woman once, odds are he will do it again. The same thing happens with people who love to argue. They will bicker and fight repeatedly. There is NEVER a reason to scream, yell and/or raise your voice to a fever pitch to get your point across.

Be someone who does Not React in the moment but has learned to step back and analyze a situation before deciding whether the issue at hand is worth a response.

Wonderful words by Ralph Waldo Emerson:

"Write it on your heart that every day is the best day in the year, He is rich who owns the day, and no one owns the day who allows it to be invaded with fret and anxiety. Finish every day and be done with it. You have done what you could. Some blunders and absurdities, no doubt crept in. Forget them as soon as you can, tomorrow is a new day; begin it well and serenely, with too high a spirit to be cumbered with your old nonsense. This new day is too dear, with its hopes and invitations, to waste a moment on the yesterdays."

"Life is to be enjoyed, not endured." (Gordon B. Hinckley)

2) It is never too late to live Happily ever after.

"You have brains in your head. You have feet in your shoes. You can steer yourself any direction you choose." (Dr. Seuss)

As of this writing, I am seventy-eight years young. I am aware that we are all going to die. For this reason, I believe in enjoying every second I have left before I breathe my last breath. I am convinced that it is never too late to make the rest of your life the best of your life.

Genetics play a role in your odds of being happy. Genetics determine two crucial factors: looks and intellect. If you are lucky enough to have both, you are fortunate. Studies have shown that people with above average looks are handed better opportunities than those with average looks. That top percent who possess striking good looks are lucky.

Most of us who reside in the middle are also lucky, but in areas that matter more. Looks eventually fade where other areas of your life usually grow.

The same goes for those gifted with a higher intellect, unlike the rest of us who reside somewhere in the middle. Then there are those at the bottom of the intelligence totem pole who must work harder to gain momentum in life. They must find what they "love" to do which will give them satisfaction, no matter how insignificant it may seem to others.

My curiosity about genetics and intellect occurred when I became a dad to a daughter with down syndrome. She is without a doubt at the bottom of the gene pool with her limited abilities to process her thoughts or logically understand them.

Watching Mary's daily routine, I am frequently reminded that ignorance truly can be blissful whereas genius can interfere in one's pursuit of happiness. Complex and/or overthinking things makes it difficult to relax, be calm and enjoy every minute.

Though looks and intellect can play a part in one's success, what is most important is discovering what makes you happy and then going full speed ahead in that direction.

This happened for me at an early age after seeing a Dean Martin and Jerry Lewis movie. I knew from that day on I wanted to be in show business. I was not sure what form of show business but that did not matter. I knew I would have to somehow set sail in that direction, and nothing was going to stop me.

Success is not the key to happiness, but Happiness is the key to success. Waking up every morning with a smile on my face ready to enjoy each day to the fullest is my idea of success. And you do not have to be great looking, super smart or rich and famous to achieve this goal. The most money I have ever earned in a year was $66,000, and yet I live a life of luxury, thanks to lucky and shrewd financial decisions.

I have a friend who for years had been unhappy in her quest for success. Her feelings of failure were due mostly to her living her life on a Merry-go-round, afraid to get off and risk. She needed to get on a Roller Coaster which would provide excitement rather than the "Groundhog Day" existence she was living.

Being on a Roller coaster with its ups and downs would likely lead to change and adventure, but the risks scared her, keeping her in a rut.

If you feel in a rut, get out of your bubble, and explore the world outside, otherwise you will miss much of the fun life has to offer. Think about how you want to spend your life… Apologizing? Regretting? Questioning? Hating yourself? Confused? Afraid to love? Not letting yourself be loved?

You need to be brave. To believe in your worth. To take a chance to grow. To take risks. You have this one life. Make yourself proud. Be the person you want to be. Be the person who will make others happy. But most importantly be the person who will make YOU happy.

3) "Change" is Growth.

"They always say time changes things, but you actually have to change them yourself." (Andy Warhol)

I am amazed how many people think Change will disrupt the stability of their lives in a negative way. Stability is nice but does not ensure HAPPINESS and usually leads to boredom. However, If you are happy and content in your present state, there would be no need to change.

But how many people are completely satisfied with their lot in life? Or feel no need for growth in their career or personal life?

I am NOT and I doubt anyone else is 100% satisfied. Every day should be a pursuit of Growth, no matter how small. Growth is a result of change. Without change, you stagnate, and most people do not do well in such a state.

I am not suggesting you should completely change your lifestyle. If You LOVE your Job, family, partner, where you live, there is NO reason for a major change.

However, if you are in a relationship which lacks passion or love and you have given it your every EFFORT or if you have a job, you know has little future, you shouldn't be afraid of CHANGE

However, if you are in a relationship which lacks passion or love and you have given it your every EFFORT or if you have a job, you know has little future, you shouldn't be afraid of CHANGE. CHANGE has always been exciting to me. Every time I move into a new direction, I learn more about myself and discover added information about the world I live in. I consider CHANGE to be an ADVENTURE into a SEA of KNOWLEDGE.

Years ago, I moved from the CITY to the COUNTRY from the smog and congestion. The move was a LEARNING experience, befriending new people with points of views different from my friends in the city.

In my new home on three acres, I gained knowledge from new experiences. I planted fruit trees and learned how to operate a backhoe which I used to construct my driveways and dig out ponds. I relished the serenity of feeding fish in my ponds and had no idea how much enjoyment this CHANGE would bring.

Similarly, I loved the CHANGE with having a daughter with Down syndrome. I had already experienced raising a normal daughter, so a new set of challenges was ahead for me, and I was ready and willing. My Down daughter is now twenty-four and the lessons, education, and growth I acquired having her is beyond measure.

These new challenges added to my GROWTH as a HUMAN BEING. When you have continued growth in your life, attaining a happy space within yourself is easier.

"The more you have, the more there is to dust"... is one way to describe why this short life we get to enjoy should not be used dusting when you can have fun.

"If I saw a child being abused, I would do everything in my power to stop it but for some ungodly reason, god won't." (Murray Langston)

4) Helping those less fortunate than us is only fair.

HOEs feel it is our duty to make the world a better place for everyone.

I have friends who do not give money to the homeless, believing they will use it to buy drugs or alcohol. I give regardless of how they plan to spend the money because the fact I am in a better situation than they are, is reason enough.

Do some poor take advantage of the system by cheating to secure welfare, food stamps and other forms of government assistance? Absolutely.

Do some Rich take advantage of the system with attorneys, accountants, lobbyists, and friends in high places to cheat the system?

Absolutely. And which group do you think has the larger negative impact on the nation's financial situation? Common sense tells me, the wealthy steal a larger piece of Americas wealth.

There are wealthy people who live a life of altruism helping wherever they can, but unfortunately, they are in the minority. Sadly, studies have shown that the wealthier you become, the greedier you become.

One of my friends of 50 years, a wealthy republican, told me he worked hard for his money and does not believe he should have to share it with those that are not as successful because they didn't work as hard.

This line of thinking is wrong. My friend, a white guy raised by parents who could afford to send him to college, was fortunate to have a dad who helped him develop drive and ambition which led to his success.

He did not grasp that his upbringing was superior to 95% of his peers and put him in a category which others would have to struggle more than he did to reach his position.

I once asked him if he was broke and entered a 2-man race where the winner would get $10,000.

But the person competing against him had only one leg, would it be fair for him to keep the entire $10,000 or should he share it? He did not have an answer when the answer is obvious.

Can you imagine if every Sunday, every person who attended church, instead bought food, and took it to the homeless. If instead of going to church, they visited kids in hospitals and brought them a book or a toy. If instead of church, visited convalescent homes and spent time chatting and joking with our elders.

If instead of church, sought out those who suffered tragedies and offered help to restore their lives. If instead of going to church to worship an imaginary God in an expensive building filled with costly artifacts, met with each other in an open space or park and built a relationship with their fellow humans by giving their time and money to help those less fortunate than them.

Can you imagine?

As previously mentioned, if you own a house and a car, you are financially in the top 1% of the almost 8 billion people in the world.
I am in that 1% and it is unquestionably a fantastic place to be... so what right do I have to look down on anyone who was unable to achieve what I have.

The only reason I am in a better position than most is because I have been LUCKIER and that is it. Lucky to have been born in a "Free" Country, lucky to have had parents who loved me, Lucky to have had a decent education, lucky to have been born healthy, lucky to be gifted with logical thinking. It has all been luck and I will forever be grateful for that luck and do not feel any jealousy of those who have been luckier than me.

I **do** believe in **"angels"**. Not heavenly angels, but earthly angels. They are those selfless human beings who go above and beyond in their efforts to care of those less fortunate than themselves. I wish I could say I have been one of them, but I have not. But I have known a few and they are truly special.

I am proud that I have lived my words. In my twenties, I went from selling shoes to performing on the Sonny & Cher show and felt a need to share my newfound success with those less fortunate. I volunteered to help mentally challenged kids and spent a year helping in my spare time. (A coincidence that years later, I would have a mentally challenged daughter)

Eventually, I collaborated with a boy named Alan Cook whose parents were killed in a trailer explosion and was mentally challenged from brain injuries he suffered from that same explosion. As my success continued, I turned my garage into a small apartment and had Alan move so he could have a better life. Later, I helped him land a job as a handyman in a retirement home where he eventually moved into. After I had children, our relationship became sporadic, limited to holidays and occasional visits but 60 years later, we still stay connected.

Live for yourself and you will live in vain; Live for others, and you will live again." (Bob Marley)

"Money is the most envied, but the least enjoyed. Health is the most enjoyed, but the least envied." (Charles Caleb Colton)

5) Living a healthy lifestyle is a priority.

Everyone should strive to be Rich... Rich in knowledge, Rich in adventure, Rich in love, Rich in friendships, Rich in laughter, and especially Rich in Health. LIFE will always be more rewarding having health, knowledge and friends than having money, gold, or diamonds.

Your health is so more Valuable than gold, Diamonds, or millions of dollars, yet people will destroy their health trying to get gold, diamonds, or Millions of dollars. It's a shame that when most of us learn how to make the most out of Life, most of it is gone. We can all agree that if you discover you have a terminal illness, everything you thought was important suddenly loses all meaning. Your job, car, house, bank account, everything you worked hard for loses all value. Why? Because the only thing that has real value is your health.

We need to spend more time staying healthy than we do becoming wealthy. It is amazing how sick people will do anything to feel better, except give up the thing that is making them sick. Most people have the "Desire" to be healthy but do not possess the "Discipline".

I do not understand why people refer to those who take care of themselves as "Health Nuts". It is a moniker of which I am proud. America has 5% of the world's population yet uses 75% of the world's prescription drugs. If you are constantly putting processed, toxic food into your body, you will be part of that 75%.

Listen to your body. It really does know best. Eat when you are hungry. Rest when you are tired. Relax when you are stressed. Take a nap when you are overwhelmed. Another thing which will add years to your life is a good night's sleep.

I believe our "minds" can be destructive to our immune system. Especially TV commercials which relay messages to our brain that we may be feeling minor aches, nausea, itchiness, dryness, or an occasional twitch.

These ads try to convince us the end is near if we do not take their drug. I am waiting for a new drug which will help us to control our blinking. Reading about health issues on the internet can be worse. Compare your body to car. A car **is** designed to run on gasoline. Our bodies were designed to run on nutritional foods such as fruits. vegetables, along with fish, poultry, and meat.

Don't you think that if you put sugar, cereal, milkshakes, or ketchup in your gas tank, it might have a negative impact on how your car runs?

If you agree, don't you think putting sugar, cereal, milkshakes, ketchup, and other processed foods loaded with chemicals, preservatives along with ingredients unbeknownst to us, that our bodies might also begin to run poorly. If you think logically, the answer is unequivocally "Yes".

As mentioned, I am seventy-eight, have not had a cold, disease or illness in 45 years and do not take any kind of drug. I still have the same energy I had in my thirties and plan to live a long time.

"Where there is love there is life" - (Ghandi)

6) Love is the answer to most our problems...

HOEs believe that all you have to do if you want to be loved is love. When you give love, odds are you will be loved in return. Every day should be spent on Loving. Loving your day, loving your partner, loving your family, Loving your job, Loving your friends, Loving your life. Being a loving person does not come from prayer or books. It comes from being a caring human being.

I am not talking about romantic love between a couple who decide life without each other wouldn't be fun, especially the naked part. You know you're in Love when you want to be together forever.

If you don't feel that way you should not allow your relationship to become serious.

Falling in love does not require much work. Staying in love does. Love will last when you convince your lover they are a priority in your life. And no two people are alike, so always appreciate the similarities and respect the differences.

Being in Love is simple. If you are NOT continually making each other happy, you are NOT in love. Love happens when your lover's happiness becomes more important than your happiness. I never realized this until I had kids and all the selfishness I had possessed ended abruptly. That same feeling should exist when you encounter your true love.

If you are not happy being single, you won't be happy being with someone. Better than falling in love with someone beautiful is falling in love with someone who makes your life beautiful. Never fall in love with someone's words. Fall in love with their actions. If you must beg someone to be in your life, they don't belong there.

People say Love Hurts but that is not true.

When someone says they love someone who does not love them, that is wrong. I believe love does not exist unless it is shared by two people. A relationship ending can hurt, Loneliness hurts, rejection hurts, losing someone hurts. People get these hurts confused with Love when Love is what makes someone feel wonderful again.

Money is responsible for more relationships ENDING and Laughter is responsible for more relationships LASTING. Good relationships do not just happen. They take time, patience and two people who genuinely want to be together. Love is an addiction to someone who makes you feel good in myriad ways, their looks, sexuality, smell, body, smile, sense of humor, intellect, the way they look at you, please you, treat you. Love is like a drug and if it's the right person, you will get addicted.

However, as I have aged, I will take Comfort over Passion in a relationship. Less complicated, less anxiety and less hurt overall. As you get older, you realize it is more important having someone hold your hand than your private parts.

And do not confuse friendships with acquaintances. The difference is acquaintances are people you like but cannot rely on... Friends are people you love and can always rely on.

Sadly, there really is no such thing as living happily ever after. Unless two lovers die together, every relationship will have a sad ending. Whether one cheats, or leaves or dies, a sad ending is eventual, and we should prepare for that sad outcome.

Life may not be always easy, but a bottle of wine, a resolute lover and stimulating conversation make it easier.

"Wealth consists not in having great possessions, but in having few wants." (Epictetus)

"Your Naked Body should only belong to those who fall in Love with your Naked Soul." (Charlie Chaplin)

7) Appreciate and enjoy every aspect of our Sexuality.

Religions, want to limit the amount of sex we engage in, not to mention how we engage in it. HOEs believe if lovers are consenting adults, whatever turns them both on and is not harmful should be enjoyed.

When my daughter reached her teen years and I had "that" talk with her, I told her as I pointed my forefinger to my brain, "The more you connect up here" followed by pointing to my groin area, "the more you will connect down there."

Without a doubt, the most important sex organ is the brain and love is the aphrodisiac.

Sex will keep you young in more ways than one.

I have discovered from my limited research when you cease having orgasms, you age more quickly. The singular, most important purpose for humans and all other species is to procreate, which can only be executed if engaged in sexual activity. When we experience orgasms, our bodies react mentally and physiologically keeping us vibrant and younger. When we cease to procreate, (have orgasms) our bodies react by aging faster, sensing we are no longer useful.

And one more important sex fact. If you cannot be silly during sex, you are not fully enjoying your sex life.

"Sex is part of nature. I go along with nature"
(Marilyn Monroe)

**"Gratitude turns what we have into enough"
Aesop**

8) Always be grateful and appreciative.

It's been said you achieve Happiness when you learn to live every minute with Love and Gratitude. Gratitude is one of the most important ingredients to living a happy and fulfilled life.

It does not matter if the glass is half empty or half full. HOEs believe we should be thankful we have a glass and grateful there is something in it.

HOEs accept that not everyone can be the best at what they do but we should always have the willingness to try our best. HOEs accept that living in the middle ain't all that bad because there is less pressure, less competition, less anxiety leading to an easier road to happiness.

HOEs accept that though we may not be gifted with looks, talent or superior intellect and will never become millionaires, we are still better off than millions in the world who live in countries where looks, talent and/or intellect are meaningless.

Most often, the things we take for granted, someone else is dreaming of. Life is wonderful when you realize that though you may have little, you have so much. HOEs have learned that it is useless to complain and appreciate all we have, especially health, friends, family, love, laughter and happiness.

We've learned that it's best to stay away from people who complain about everything and appreciate nothing. We've learned to never compare our lives to others. Your journey is what matters.

We've learned to never take ourselves seriously because seriously, no one else does.

We've learned to enjoy the fruits of our labor rather than wait until the fruit starts going bad.

We've learned to only keep things that are beautiful, useful, or joyful; To burn the good candles, use the nice sheets and don't save things for a special occasion because every day is a special occasion.

We've learned to never be jealous of those richer or more successful.

"Too many people want what other people have without doing what other people have done" (Travis Robertson)

"It's not WHAT we have in our life, but WHO we have in our life that counts." (J.M. Laurence)

9) Never judge people on Color, Race, Religion, Gender, or Sexuality. Judge people on whether they're an Asshole.

HOEs believe we should not concentrate on raising our kids to have more than we have but to be happier than we are.

A study conducted by the University of Chicago found that children raised in non-religious households are kinder and more altruistic than those raised with religion. The study, published in the journal, Current Biology looked at 1170 children between the ages of 5 and 12 years in six countries (Canada, China, Jordan, Turkey, USA, and South Africa) examined "The religiousness of their household, and parent-reported child empathy and sensitivity to justice."

Across all countries, parents in religious households reported their children expressed more empathy and sensitivity for justice in everyday life than non-religious parents.

The study states: "Our findings contradict the popular assumption that children from religious households are more altruistic and kinder toward others. In our study, kids from Atheist and non-religious families were more generous," said Prof. Jean Decety, who led the study.

According to the study, the findings did not change much over time and children raised in religious households did not follow the natural trend of being more giving with age but that they were the least likely to share. The study is not a shock to parents who raise kids outside religion.

From my observations, caring, loving kids are a result of caring, loving parents, regardless of whether they were raised with or without religion.

"Children must be taught How to think... not What to think." (Margaret Mead)

"Religious wars are basically people killing each other over who has the better imaginary friend." (Napoleon Bonaparte)

10) When religion and the love of god are replaced with education and the love of humanity, the world will be an amazing place.

Teaching kids to worship themselves, their family, friends & humanity makes more sense than teaching them to worship a God which may or may not exist.

Don't you think that a loving god would want churches to be open 24/7 to feed and/or shelter the poor and disabled? If the millions of people who spend hours preparing and going to churches to worship an obviously egomaniac god, instead spent those millions of hours helping the poor, that would be a religion to consider?

Religion is **Junk Food** for the mind. It might give temporary satisfaction hoping you'll see your family after you die when you go to an imaginary heaven, but like junk food, it is basically harmful, lacking intellectual nutrition.

The Real Question is Not "where" Civilization began but "when" will it begin? (Anonymous}

CHAPTER FIVE

On the Gun issue

"Until we stop harming all other living beings, we are still savages." (Thomas Edison)

I previously mentioned that my goal has changed from enjoying every day to enjoying every minute. Sadly today, I believe the reason you should enjoy every minute is that at any moment, you could get shot. I do not understand why Americans (hunters not included) need to own guns, especially assault weapons. I spent five years in the military where I shot guns and have NEVER been so afraid of my fellow Americans, I felt a need to own a gun for protection.

I was once robbed at gunpoint and was glad I did not have a gun which may have resulted in one or both of us being killed. Statistics show that if you keep a gun in your home, the odds of someone you know, or love being killed by that gun are 1,000 times higher than a crazed person breaking into your home and killing you.

Sure, it could happen, but the odds of lightning killing you are higher.
Please do not resort to the second amendment argument which was written to protect us from OUR Government. The chance of our government turning on us is ridiculous and if they did, civilians would not have a chance against the arsenal of weapons the U.S. military has. How can anyone say we live in a civilized country when so many feel the need to own guns to protect themselves from each other.

CHAPTER SIX

HOE TIPS

"If you are depressed, you are living in the past. If you are anxious, you are living in the future. If you are at peace, you are living in the present."
- Lao Tzu

Never, never TIPS to living happily ever after...

-Never wallow in debt. Pay off your bills asap. Owing money makes you a SLAVE to whoever you owe it to. If you can, pay off your house asap (which I did 30 years ago) and I always paid cash for a car. I have never had a car payment. I cannot say enough how easy life becomes when you have no monthly mortgage or car payment.

-Never let anyone occupy space in your mind who does not deserve to be there. Rid your mind of negative people asap.

-Never allow yourself to be bored. The opposite of happiness is boredom, so keep your mind and body active every day, if you want health and prosperity to come your way. Boredom is the cancer of happiness. People who say they are bored, are usually boring people. Do not be one of them.

-Never concentrate on "what" you have in life, but "who" you have in life. Happiness has so much to do with the people you surround yourself.

-Never worry about how you are going to "die". Concentrate on how you are going to "live". You only live once" is a false statement. You live every day; you only die once.

-Never "Overthink". Too many people ruin their enjoyment of TODAY by Over Worrying about TOMORROW. There might be a reason or two to be unhappy but if you open your eyes to the world around you, there are thousands of reasons to be happy. Life is simple. Whatever makes you feel bad, get rid of it. Whatever makes you feel good, keep it.

-Never concern yourself with problems you have little control over. Constantly voicing your opinion about politics may make you feel connected, but if you allow them to make you angry, you are wasting energy. If you are serious about political issues, get into the arena where you can affect change by becoming a politician. Otherwise, if you are worried more about the world's problems than you are about your own problems, you are going to have a tough time enjoying life. Your problems are much easier to solve.

The phrase, "in 5 years will this really matter" approach to problems works for me because most problems are not that serious and are usually temporary. Time heals most everything. If you were able to see the many problems other people must deal with, you would likely not be so upset with yours.

-Never hang with negative people who think the opposite of the way you do. Being with like-minded people is much more conducive to being happy than being with opposite minded people.

-Never put off until tomorrow things that can make you happy today. Too many people wait all week for the weekend, all year for summer, and all their lives for happiness.

-Before going to sleep, try to think of the thing that made you happiest that day no matter how small... and do it again.

And remember...to always be with someone who makes you happy. (Now remove the word with)

And remember...the most important thing you will ever learn in life is how to be your own best friend.

And remember...there is nothing better than a friend, unless it is a friend with ice cream or wine.

And remember the things that contribute to happiness most are Not Things.

Never, Never Tips on relationships, life and love

-Never stay in a non-loving relationship to avoid being alone.

-Never miss an opportunity to tell those you love that you love them.

-Never allow Emotionally draining friendships and/or relationships to continue.

-Never allow the one you love to feel alone, especially when you are with them.

-Never use angry words when you are in a bad mood. You will change your mood often, but you cannot replace angry words.

-Never leave someone "wondering" how you feel about them because it is honestly the worst thing you could do to a person.

-Never **text** about personal problems. Texts can be misunderstood when lacking expression. Discuss relationship issues in person or by phone.

-Never allow people to make you feel stupid and remember, people will treat you the way you let them.

-Never try to get people to change who don't want to.

-Never excuse mistreatment and dysfunctional behavior by saying, "That's just how they are."

-Never be afraid to be eccentric, different, or unique

-Never overcommit to things you really do not want to do.

-Never be unhappy about a sad ending. Be happy about a new beginning.

-Never say, "Those were the days"... say, "These are the days.

-Never dwell on coulda, woulda, shoulda... focus on, can do, will do, and need to.

And...never let anyone push you around... unless you're in a shopping cart cause that shit is fun.

"IF" TIPS to accepting Change...

-If you are trying your best, that is what really matters.

-If you are not having fun at work, you need to find another job.

-If you would keep your job if you stopped getting paid, you are on the road to success

-If you feel like a loser, remember... you are the sperm that won.

-If you want something and you don't have it, it means you didn't want it bad enough.

-If something excites you, do something about it, do Not put it on a back burner.

-If "Shit happens", flush the toilet and move on.

-If you want to believe in something, believe that the future can be better than the present and that you have the power to make it so.

If you want to fear something, Fear being in the exact same place today as you were last year.

"IF" Tips to live by...

-If you cannot say something nice about someone, shut the fuck up.

-If a person is nice to you but is not nice to the waiter, that person is an asshole.

-If you think certain people suck, do not spend time with them.

-If someone tells you bad things about other people, you better believe they will be saying bad things about you to other people.

-If you try helping an asshole, all you will get in return is shit.

-If you cannot make certain people like, love, understand, accept or be nice to you. Good news is... It does not matter one bit.

"Intelligence is the ability to adapt to change." (Stephen Hawking)

And remember...

"Failure" is NOT the opposite of success; it is a part of success.

Life is about kicking ass, not kissing it.

A life without Passion is a life without much life.

The only person who can hold you back... is you

Stop saying I wish and start saying I will.

Every problem is a gift which helps us grow.

Your job will **not** take care of you when you are sick. Your friends and family will... so stay in touch with them.

When going after what you love in life, never take "NO" for an answer.

AND...

Four words which will lead you in the right direction... Explore. Love. Experience. Create.

There are five types of people you want to surround yourself with: the inspired, the passionate, the motivated, the grateful and the open minded.

"The color of one's skin should be as irrelevant as the length of one's hair." (Alejandro G. Iñárritu)

CHAPTER SEVEN

Rules and Questions

My twelve rules for living a long life...

1) Never allow your desire to attain wealth be a priority over your desire to maintain your health.

2) Never let anyone who has done you wrong cause you to do what is not right.

3) Never allow a disagreement to turn into an intense argument.

4) Never ignore loving words or loving arms.

5) Never miss an opportunity to enjoy a good laugh at yourself.

6) Never let a day pass without doing at least one thing that makes you happy.

7) Never avoid "Change" which always leads to growth.

8) Never stop learning about stuff that interests you.

9) Never cease to be amazed and grateful for your life.

10) Never stop telling those you love that you love them.

11) Never worry about dying or anything else you have no control over.

12) Never stop living in the NOW. The past is gone, the future uncertain so enjoy the NOW and Don't just Exist in it, LIVE in IT to the max.

10 Questions to ask yourself:

1) What is your job and what job would you rather be doing?

2) Can you pinpoint the best day of your life?

3) If you could only eat one meal every day, what would it be?

4) What two things are you good at?

5) What two things are you great at?

6) What two things are you bad at?

7) What is the number one thing to do on your bucket list?

8) What is the ONE Thing you believe is missing from your life?

9) What one thing do you believe has a negative impact on your happiness.

10) If you could close your eyes right now, open them and be anywhere in the world, where would you be?

My answers:

1) I am in creative arts and do not want another job.

2) The day I was born.

3) King crab legs, rice, corn on the cob and a salad.

4) Making people laugh and being a friend.

5) Being happy and being a dad.

6) Repairing a car and being religious.

7) Make the ones I love happy.

8) A romantic relationship.

9) The state of U.S. politics.

10) Right where I am.

These answers give me an awareness of what I feel about my life now and what changes could make it better. 8 and 9 could use improvement but the others signal all is great.

IN CONCLUSION

"Why do people always say God Bless America? Why can't they say God Bless the World?" This quote by comedian George Carlin says volumes about how religion divides rather than unites. With an estimated 4,200 different religions in the world, all professing they are the one, how can any thinking person think any one of them is worth thinking about.

Since 9/11, I have frequently heard the phrase that Science flies people to the moon. Religion flies people into skyscrapers. It is true. The reality is religion has been responsible for more wars, murder, death, destruction, and humanity would have been much better off without it.

I never understood when my religious friends would tell me that I should be **"god fearing".** I would reply, I would rather be **"life loving"**. If god was real, why would he want you to fear him. Shouldn't he want to be your friend? God as depicted in the bible is **not** a nice guy?

If you believe the bible, god is jealous and vengeful and blind obedience is the only thing that will end his murderous and destructive ways. Would a loving god kill most of the world's population as he did in the great flood, saving only Noah and his tribe of doubles?

If god was the inspiration for the bible, then he is hateful and evil, having people stoned or burnt alive, killing thousands for their sins and commanding his own people to wipe out entire cities. Entire books have been devoted to violence in the bible.

God's anger and wrath is displayed throughout the bible, invoking the death penalty for paltry "crimes" against him, ordering death for working on the Sabbath, rebelliousness of a child, premarital sex and the requirement for a priest to burn his daughter alive if she became a prostitute (Leviticus 21:9). God's punishment seems harsh, unjust, and disproportionate. How could any thinking person consider this to be a god of mercy and love?

Mel Gibson's movie, "The Passion of the Christ," a huge box office success was one of the most despicable, violent, and inhumane films I have ever tried watching and should be considered child abuse if shown to children, which was mandatory in many religious families.

Unicorns are mentioned nine times in the bible and cats are not mentioned at all. This alone should tell you how legit the bible is!

Finally, it is the culmination of my beliefs which have contributed to my living like I am already in heaven and it is up to the reader to determine whether they are in line with what I believe.

If you do **not** connect with my beliefs, I wish you all the best in finding your path along life's journey.

If you **are**, join me in living not only every day, but every minute with a smile on your face.

Until we meet again... Stay Healthy – Stay Strong – Stay Silly - Stay Happy – Stay loving.

REMEMBER:

1) Eat Healthy.

2) Be trustful and Honest.

3) Follow your dreams.

4) Be passionate about your work.

5) Be patient.

6) Judge less.

7) Smile often.

8) If you are able, exercise regularly and take frequent walks.

9) Learn to Relax or Meditate.

10) Love yourself.

11) Forgive easily.

12) Be grateful.

13) Be Disciplined.

14) Think positive.

15) Use alcohol/drugs moderately.

16) Believe in yourself.

17) Keep an open mind.

18) Don't make excuses.

19) Be kind/Speak well of others.

20) Talk less/listen more.

21) Enjoy each day.

22) Avoid comparing yourself to others.

23) Look at failure as opportunity.

24) Never allow anyone to keep you from moving forward.

25) Pick friends who are smarter/more successful than you.

26) Let go of your past mistakes and/or past hurts.

27) Sleep well.

28) Get rid of negative people.

29) Always have something to look forward to, something to do, someone to love, and Something to hope for.

30) Be more concerned about being a loving and valuable person than being Rich and Powerful. But if you can be both, that's a good thing.

Made in the USA
Middletown, DE
21 November 2022